Under the War and Other Poems

UNDER THE WAR
AND OTHER POEMS

Arthur Sale

HUTCHINSON OF LONDON

Hutchinson & Co (Publishers) Ltd
3 Fitzroy Square, London W1

London Melbourne Sydney Auckland
Wellington Johannesburg Cape Town
and agencies throughout the world

First published 1975

Set in Linotype Baskerville

Printed in Great Britain by
Flarepath Printers Ltd, St. Albans, Herts
and bound by Wm Brendon & Son Ltd
Tiptree, Essex

ISBN 0 09 123170 1

Contents

UNDER THE WAR

Existence seemed a mighty crack
To make me visible.

Emily Dickinson

Renovation

Amateurs built it years ago,
each wall with a different stagger,
sobered up by professionals
with plumblines and diagonals,
and plaster straitwaistcoats disguise
acute angles from the most upright gaze.

Today I connive to renovate
masks that level lack and surfeit,
an amateur to decorate
venal attempts to put to right
what amateurs did wrong slipshod
in many a delicate pastel shade.

Rehardened by enhanced case
whited or tinted sepulchres
reeled from the brush so that dusk could
coincident so merge discord
with the hour for public show. Am I too
professional I wonder for an amateur?

But tradesman's craft and mine differ,
his nonchalance is my fear
of general reckoning and review.
"Yet why? The renovation does you
credit, I like that ceiling cream,
and all looks solid, solid as rock."

Behind your back in every room,
clean through the clean sheet of every room,
look where the black cancelling crack
upstarts erect the deep foundation crime.

The Snag

"How pleasant a bungalow, such curved glass
and roughcast not
too rough, good looking like nut
gobbets on cakes, not overclose
the lane, and such a gloss

on pane and paint in the afternoon sun,
inside so light
so modern, would you sell it?"
I'd say no but for one reason
or yes but for one reason

that makes no the only honest answer.
You see this hand,
dripping with plaster and behind
that wrinkled bleached and sore –
a washerwoman's ce-

ment makes hands. You see that crack, I ram
in it cement
and plaster enough, times out of mind,
to fill not a hole but a whole room
and always there is room.

Or if the master crack's bottomless pit
seems to be full
of substitutes there is no fail
starting like parasite or pet
for a sustaining pat.

The more I survey cracks the less their ways
make sense, yet pour
my all in them despite despair
of consolidants that make worse
distension expending their power with ours.

The Mist

As the infinite series of recurrent dream
sidles to its interminable terminus
the endless train draws up along the endless platform
but never close enough to stop,
it must, surely it must, fouling at the Nth term the point
    the limiting sum
and quietly leaving the rails—look I have
returned escaped, I am awake and never changed.

And while outside the mist lasts nothing is changed, no lost
ticket's recurrent number is missed, for the mist
blocking yet opening out the twi-casemented window
into a decreasingly truncated cone
sucks like a conjuror's hat into its adaptable envelope of
    vacuum
the protracted ordinates of dream, and even
even before involuntary eyes can bear the dragging
abyss, the dreaded opening lesson of the day,
and the chronic pain turn over, painlessly
the painful pressure root of the recurrent crack
opening above and below the window
(as if the wall should be cracked and not the picture on it)
is drawn out by undroning suction, or at least the nerve is
    numbed.

And in this tranquil
O so freshly mopped clean discharge of guilt a house
inveterately divided against itself, settled
down into comfortable halves, into a separation
mutual and unrancorous, is a solution
as acceptable and unremarkable as a halved cake, while
the mist holds soft possession and the strong impression no
crack can grind its edges on my heart.

Relief is now the signature rippling across the wall
and even the void glass interval cannot void it,
for along the inset graphlines with quick change of plane
  and plan
and a carte-blanche ticket to infinity flashing
from indefinity it rejoins at the top of the window
the crack line regiment it never left, but where
trick-riding its asymptote it returns –
changing surely state not train –
is unplottable as the point of awakening, impossible
as to bring the crack's wry planes to one table: no
matter now for now
the crack sides keep the general peace
(while mist persists and vacuum holds) not cheek by jowl
but by the defile and abyss between them,
definitive issue and resolve of forces, and
scrawl on the wall, though touching on infinity, is
(unlike Balshazzar's) harmless because legible,
as the sickeningly seamless uncrackable crib of neurosis
yawns with relief at the simple recalled combination,
until
only just until the reticulate mist haul off, call
its pipistrell decoy in,
the gin.

The Tree

"The tree I remember best, the hollow
an eyesore, unofficial public dump
to fill the pond, once skatable, called 'Reedy'.
But the elm tree hardly saw, roots drove clean under,
such rammle. It stood back high – "   It stood across
my French windows, so close they opened on it.
"Fell, I suppose, missing the house, luckily
a low one? Elms are treacherous on this galt
bedrocked on subterranean lakes."   No, cut.
"It came to that? Took no doubt more than due
of what sunshine was going?"   Almost too high
and too high-branched to shade it.   "Spoilt the view
from the wide windows?"   No view except in winter
(We made the hedge grow tall), in winter only
of rotten sheds, roofs for the rats' holes, and,
sole relic of its shed, a turnip cutter.
"If less view was no loss, why must the tree fall?"
Because the bungalow's foundation was
lodged on the broad back of one of the roots.
"Sounds safe – an extra beam to bear the house,
or keel to ride the laminal underland sea."
A knife to slice the house through like a cake.
That tree, bent to the gale like a full sail
spread miles, dangerous vibrating miles, above
the squat safe house, by infinitesimal
displacement, a tremor through the roots, could, would,
snap the house clean as a clay pipe stem.   "True
as seismograph a house might be what most
could be desired – except the cost. So roost
must fall in case the rooster should. I see
more in the danger than in the solution.
A rip-saw spitting through that root had saved
a day's grunt at the trunk, the house, the tree."
Too late to think of that. Besides, the tree
was too grand for the house, made it look mean.

Besides, I like, yes I do like, to see
the turnip cutter chop the winter sun
brought close by frost and brightened like a mangold.
"One can buy safety at too low a price."
Not if it is safety, but safety has
a shell-proof shelter lies lower than truth
and as unvenial.   "You mean – ?"   I mean
look at my house with low safe precautions
leaded and shelled and underpinned and cracked
neat as an egg on a basin rim, spilt gold,
and irrecoverable as Humpty Dumpty.

The Tell-Tale Crack

The face is fair enough to outward view
with long eyes, despite jowl
underslung and nose askew,
straight, but too like a girl
lashed, hair a rose gall

above brow high broad beautifully modelled:
after a walk or wash
the long face is unstaled
from sedentary ash.
What more could a man wish

of moderate hope? What flawmarks of the lash
on uncleft chin and smooth
soft skin, heart's flagellat-
ions' wounds and wales? What, none? – Nor truth
from the loose wealed and breached mouth.

In Nature Too

Abandoned the square bungalow, I follow
the low level lane to the high highroad,
which, being Roman, is dead straight and dead,
but which my lane loops off as naturally
but resolutely as a caterpillar
eluding enemies by twig illusion.

The concrete obstruction of the tank traps foiled,
uphill my own height almost in my own height
forcing, from the sharp highroad spine I see
the west flowing bank on bank before me,
spiralling flatly to the arched cloud springing
from two round haystacks stocky as bulls,
caissons too solid for their temporary bridge.

And now the picture in the frame: for ground,
plough lipping pasture in a sweeping bite,
terraced on which, trees like a palimpsest
of amphitheatres on inclining axes,
– erased except for elongated parcels
in lunes and lenses, slivers, crescents, belt
upon ribboned belt, tone after tone of
greens greys browns blurring in the cloud, itself
the colour of blued suds after hard service,
and a wash of mist to fix the *genius loci*
emanating from the hedgerow chestnuts,
dark domes deployed across the level foreground.

The composition waited, waited for what?
Something was incomplete, was the keystone
forgotten, or the figure for the scale?
Not me, though some formation in me longed
to be precipitated on that wet earth or
accepted by those dense and beavered sentries
like a mist bleb welling under a bough.

Not me, that dewy silvan Eden was
too tender, pristine, inlaid, prenatal
for my sharp sides. For my young son maybe,
but sleep had curved him in his proper Eden
ridging out others not too dark although
too pure to see. Undisclosed in his pram
his swaddled unresponsive crescent, but
now like an afterthought, inevitable
but unsurprising, that, illuminating,
happily solves, all, without the least to-do
slicing itself a segment from the very
pitch of the cloud arch, a sudden 'Judas' open,
at home like Gunnar singing through his cairn,
the crescent moonlight on the final scene
presides, complacent deus ex machina,
subsides, into and with its bridge into the
rising the motionless whirlpool of trees.

Noah Stylites

Those brisk and roric walks, unnecessary
aperitifs before the porridge, grapefruit,
bacon and eggs, before the Second Flood
was more than a mud geysir in the East,
a resort of unwholesome fascination.

The gear laid out and kettle on the fire,
I filled my free half hour up with freedom
on empty road and path, while the lithe bitch,
disdaining scents the dew had snuffed out first,
untrodden yet by new, broke the trail for me,
her long poised tail swaying like a censer
between the live pillars of that intact Eden,
to where the old man, stub arms along the
iron bridge rail, leaned across sewage smells,
the only favours of the naked ditch,
to the green other slope, in hopes of seeing
some old drake tread an accommodating fowl –
"I seen 'em oft, me and this little maid"
(several rails down but staring just as hard).

Sometimes we'd meet him splayfoot on the path,
cursing each single stone with stick and tongue:
"The sod, as laid these pebbles without sand!
They'll ne'er bed down till winter wet, they'll be
the death o' me." He died, I saw him last
on his last walk, just crawling from a hedge
and from a fit, an independent, earthy,
oathy little man, drab face, drab clothes,
but money in the bed, a retired farmhand,
who told the farmers on his beat his mind –
Tractors too heavy for that galt, two horses
one horse too many, steam ploughs were the best.
He ran his crone round almost at his last gasp,
whose screeches fetched his sons from doors away
to haul him off.

It was then I dropped my walks,
leaned on the garden gate, the dog daring me
till habit tamed her, hailed the timid roadman,
who prowled on his safe stretch of road and talked
wisely of war, eyes busy pendulums
towards the unlikely passing of his boss.

But now the fens were flooded, I took to
latching the gate, retreated in good order
back up the garden slope, turned the big key,
and looked out from the window at the waste,
my eyes bleared by illusions of land in
the sewage crust and faces in the flotsam,
feeling the waters' impure ablution
warren like rodents in my cracked foundations
ventilating storey after storey
(as they will comb a rotted down forgotten
bean-stack into a vibrating skyscraper).

Then left the look-out unmanned, settled myself
full length on this broad comfortable settee,
and watched only cracks, how they multiply
in that Nile flood of fertilizing blood,
waxing on walls now crazy paved like a tapped
eggshell, of that neat radiating creeper
with its minute ingrown dichotomy
themselves the mere interstices shored up
by the mercurial mass of their destroyer,

walls mortared once as fondly as once Melville
stitched his thick patchwork White Jacket
(a handy house complete with airing cupboards)
for lack of the essential caulking pitch
into a mortal liability
when inside safety's buoyant fling he struggled
in its and the waves' immobilization.

The Challenges

If it were only me cracked
no matter; all you say
would be correct:
a man should struggle even to see
creation wrecked.

And verse should be gritted by
fight, and by the bind semened
which dry may be
inscrutable, but wetted a cerement
screw, of flower soft cement.

And I lack Odin's spittle, may-
be, to organize my ashes;
and admit my
reactions arouse no flood fashes,
have, good or vicious,

no futures. As they do not count
nor does your verse, you say,
and so, recant
your symbol. Mine I can, yes I
do, your world's I can't.

"*Neither fear nor courage*
saves us"

Is it enough to say that
I am a coward and the
harsh voice from the road the
gate rocking the rubber footsteps on the concrete
the dead knock on the shaking door are but
the casual visitor the baker's boy and I need
have no fear of   **?**
no fear

Is it enough to say my nerves are
bad and at night the
whispering on the road the
swishing grass outside the veiled French windows
the clear tapping on the undulating window are but
the wind the rat the scratching twig and I need
have no fear of   **?**
no fear

Is it enough to declare that
I am neurotic craven and that
all I fear is the policeman the
glasshouse the snooper the collector for
spitfires the red cross the salvage the battleships and these
    mean
the loss of cash only or freedom or life and I need
have no fear of   **?**
no fear

It is not enough to declare these
facts or these fancies
for I have heard
inside the fears and the uniformed voices a minute question
rocking our foundations splintering our entrances the
    held out
telegram by the wind or the messenger boy requiring
an answer or   **?**
no answer

AFTERNOON INTO DUTY

Against Afternoons

Waking afternoons from sleep,
however wide back the curtains slip,
the sun is never the same, so young
so glad, nor, however hot, so strong,
never anything but sad
so sad. What a lot of life has soared
dipped and gone unaccounted for
in a horizontal half hour.

But those flagging siestaless
of life are torture worse than loss.
The heart drags at its tether's end,
the eyeballs boiled and dressed with sand,
and in collision in the street
the sun is through you in a stride,
you are gone, you are atomised,
and as of men and buildings missed
(so soldiers swear) the shadow stays
in those two absent Nipon cities,
so of yourself the shadow is
loose on the solid heat, or worse,
for every grain of eye-grinding grit
separately disintegrate
leaves by a cruel oversight
of humanity one perquisite –
crackling circuits of electric pain,
by which (too big for lids) gouged open,
under the torture eyes get rid
of such importunities of road
as gate-crash their stretched and strained ring,
though your mass may like crumb and drink
have passed confirming into those.
The ears kill any buzz but theirs,
and heart's folding and shutting pull
dislocates earth's from either pole.

On not a fly- but monstrous balance-
wheel you are drawn in dizziest beelines,
for dockers', Dunkirk's, best in war
to these turn-rounds the worst strikes were.

Or else this dismal autarky
though it displace all but the key
(the key is pain) to the macrocosm
can toss the latter down its chasm
having like Alice reversed size,
or, worse, know what outside it sees
is all inside, and inside can,
turning the skin, become *its* skin.
Outside in an interior ring
is compelled by this smothering,
and inside digits each can seem
by elephantiasis the sum,
or by synecdoche disguised.

Thus spider or her absorbed guest,
the street's King Kong or lightest snack,
from Lilliput or Brobdingnag
you unexpectedly escape,
and with a river as sole curb,
which oars' gesticulations ward
enforcing like police gauntlets white,
as on the daisiest spot you stretch,
guzzling in them like an ostrich,
a miser counting them like sheep,
salvation takes the surpliced shape
of daisies, rowers, in dizzy eyes,
requiring, this leucocytosis,
only sleep, peace to fight disease.

But as for sleep you advertise, as
on silvered eyes the sun's seal lies,
first of a host, a black bacillus,
from foul congestion emigrant
of liver or of brain migrained,
invades that streaming slide, alas, and sleep.

Impotent on the daisies' lap
you despair, better they in yours?
Then both might suffer less abuse –
sleep in lieu of a white afternoon
for you, they whiter and for none.
– Or so you mumble up the straight
reassumption of the street.

O inexcusable afternoons
your cursed existence here renounce;
be struck off day's too-long regimen,
since, sleep or no sleep, you ruin mine.

A Horizontal Afternoon

I wake but cannot rise.
Though the sun, a busy all about me mellow nurse,
unfurls me warmly lubricating knees,
featherily bolsters me upright
with long strong rods and rays,
injects but sympathises, wrestles but agrees —
despite caress and prod
I cannot rise.

Though conscience is called in —
professional bonhomie and parsonic bray —
"Congratulations first on looking spry;
from such recuperative nap
no danger of a cold on
rising up, gently now . . ." — despite all that's skilled in
levitation and snoop
I stay skull down.

Approached by interest
with pencil tapping on my bedrail, can I pay
in full but if unfortunately poor
up, and the sooner the better,
for general strikes uncrossed
contract the general ataxia of the crazed —
the flatter for bread and butter
crises I rest.

Though in grand chorus, "Rise!"
sings life and fair occasion, "Rise!" sing religions
morphologies moralities delusions
diligence hygiene and the main chance —
these chants framed to rouse, drowse
me, till unknown unnamed a voice that same word "Rise!"
carelessly as it mentions
surprised I rise.

For Afternoons

Black and chalky as nuns
on a professional call,
when only hopes of tea
endure the afternoons,
upon my droning school
descends futility;

inspecting with approval
all but the somnolence –
"For frustration should be
unrestful as gravel,
neither peace nor violence
but an unrelieved stand by.

Of round the clock alerts
keyed to the warble, else
futility itself
might not put out the lights,
in the relish of its ills
its corrosives dissolve."

Though in ripest rapport
elsewhere, on afternoons
I must repudiate
as incendiary the report –
What *can* the intense inanes
of morning with the idiot

recriminations of night
from conflagration keep
(a detonation nothing
could, no, you yourself could not,
Futility, escape),
but the afternoon's nodding?

Either a breathing space,
siesta, pregnant pause,
allow like parasites
or perish with the tree
in vain co-venalty.

To save such parricides
all this accidie cedes
but losing wins the peace
by staying on to tea

Death in the Afternoon

*Death destroys a man but the idea of death
saves him* (E. M. Forster).
*A not sufficiently constant thought of death
has given an insufficient value to the tiniest
movement of your life* (A. Gide).

Half time, mid passage, half way round, Piscis
or Virgo? Widdershins anyway, but now,
reversed perversity, no longer proud.
Withered virginity, a fusty nut,
a pretty kettle of fish the sole reward
of making virtue out of finickiness.

Afternoons are stocktakings of mornings
(thirty four years worsted and wasted) and
for taking advance orders for the night.
Orders are fears for four and thirty years
(to be worsted, to be wasted?), with two
afternoon years of breathing space thrown in.

The past would not matter, I'd dump the past
in one lump sum outside the workhouse gate,
and feel no sin for talent lost, accounts
unrendered, and such clichés, despite the time,
the prodigious count of over thirty years,
to reach mere not-childhood. I'd cut my losses
with a mock-boasting parallel to the
back-forwards hero of the folk; but it's O
horror for the night, not night horror but
horror for the night, and not for its winter
incessance but midsummer vanishing point,
come, gone, and dear, like fairground final sessions.

Across still formulating afternoons
once the gong strikes, the sudden gestalt summons,
to responsibility and not to tea,
then time stops marking and filling in time;
without an interval, like trolley buses,
from rest position it out-lurches light,
"and the first minute after noon is night."

When the flash reveals responsibility
as your now first known doppelganger, every
second has its meaning to be entered, or
plunges with you like a sounding whale
gored by the barb, with speed seemingly doubled
by the contrary upbubblings of time.

Whatever words you now first know to say
and acts that now come to you to be acted,
never so many must bulge so short a time,
in cobweb corners and dark jamming drawers,
last minute harvests in flabbergasted barns.

Afternoon's prime eye-opening glimpse of death
(That known and obvious museum reconstructions
should come to life as your own Benjamin
freely acknowledged as the family face!)
is, by a Pallas Athenean section,
responsibility's head-aching birth.

It is death, not life, with salutary panic
that gives expression to time's face, races
into invisibility its fingers,
transforms the afternoon's insipid tea
into bubbling inspissation. For death
that closes eyes in fact, in preview clears them: –
from futility's matter in the corners,
the split will's squint, muddle's astigmatism,
the creeping crow-footed myopia
of interest: – sins and skins against the light,
scared now (but only till the rattle stops?)
by the enlightening vision of my own demise
(like Scrooge's trinity of ghosts in one)
its positively first appearance to me
in the fauteuils of this belated matinee.

"*This upright thwarting*"

This upright thwarting and undiquitous zeal
to fix, wedge in position, and not to
kick from that sub-zero heighted galty
Despond Pond headlong me, pulls, piles, resil-
ient down responsibility in the soil.
A weeping willow or a Judas rooty
at tips or a muddled mangrove aisle, I stay
put in a bursting world by some reprisal
that self-spites, for responsibility,
serving me with daily notice to quit,
wills the world what but honestly to restore
pillage that by burn-hole talent acquired
shall and must be? Multi-unanimous-armed duty
orders me off (a god), world hugs (a squid).

"*To move I must reverse the end*"

To move I must reverse the end
to which I move, for only the steep straddle
of the escalator's descent
(once stretches of tread collapsing into treadle
underfoot rocking treacherous stead-
y to a staircase of rock
or marble, down which dignified and staid,
or quickened by, for those who must be quick,
sinister plunges equally invested
with risk and gain, one has arrived arrived and only stood)

– only the well-greased easy world's way
could take me for a primavernal but
avernal ride, if anywhere
I could but find my duty had its beat
on those all-ways gradients to the sea
alltheway oneway packed
with a pig-a-back squeezed cars. Though only so
can be the concrete desert where I'm parked
escaped, unanimously like insane inspect-
ors duties digit me to hop-
skip up descending escalators (worst
of treadmills, still more than my hap
to date, which only consciousness of waste
exhausts, exhausting) high up, higher, highest!

No belt though it convey
the assembled globe could serve or save my haste.
To move that duty may, world not, devour
(though unless this transport, that may not deliver),
my hope, that neither may, me stranded, is my fear.

Inner and Outer Duty

Duty laughs more than flowers, liberates
from the loud-speaker vans of occupiers
announcing duties that remain invisible
although the crime of disobedience is death
and death does come from disobedience.

For though these menaces (the sole offering
loud-speaker duties bring), so amplified
the elastic core of each sound crumb is snapped
and motes float pointless and unrecognizable
like the sparse random pointillisme of
gutterpress snapshots, can be concentrated
consubstantiated into bloody flesh,
no fingers ever release the blank blinds
to show armed profiles to the convinced street.

One cannot think these conquerors have fathers
or fatherlands, and even their brutal voices
tattooing upper windows seem to re-
verberate from transparence they alarm
and façades indistinguishable from sound.

But my duty is beauty, a talented
though single flower, more inaccessible,
indifferent, dangerous, to transmontane voices
than Tibet, and than its holy heir a bud
more fortuitously inevitable;
a flower more latent furled and foiling than
the spiniest guarded of centennial cacti,
forced hydroponically by midnight sun
(crumbless my soil, non-mycorrhizal, thin),
a sudden fairy floodlit church confounding
eyes and an ingrained plague of darkness, known
for one's own, both the marvel and the horror —
to flocking duties flakless offering
that must be still illumined, still preserved.

My duty, though unique as thumbprints, only
antonymous but like banalities
(fitting as loosely as its name the church)
to those aerial droning duties speaks
("Fulfil redeem yourself, to hell those others!"),
and it, like those, carries its penalty
of death for disobedience or, worse,
a long existence knowing one is dead.

But where their suffocating sky though charged
only with lint loads the bowels like lead coils,
and though my duty's massive outward image
is Atlas shouldering all gravitation,
my heart lifts like the arrow in the fairground
under the maul, and ringing bells aloft.

TRANSFORMATIONS

The City

Peered in over the rim the city looks dried
stock in the pot. Each on its sandstone bluff,
Stylites so distant one ceases to remember
whether aloft there be mummy or statue,
castle and church lift
clear of the roofage ravelled round their base
like buckled glaciers – lamposts whose baskets hold
only their own scrap iron,
poles of a museum circuit so furred up
one ceases to remember
the city hall as the upstart demolisher – a wedge
dwarfing dislodgements as a sledgehammer its nut, a needle-
nippled Uhlan helmet of a dome tieing
tiered columns in like balanced acrobats, injecting
even into the burghers' sleep its own conception of time
that brims the basin in a single chime but cannot seep
not a rumble not a murmur
deep in the caves that, one is careless to remember,
riddle the sandstone span after span, silurian colosseums,
threaded on a mysterious fresh air, a cool
cellarage to history where our clues soon run out.

A Transformation Scene

Bidden to the christening of a heart I entered
a silver spoon
hot in my hand but my spine
prickled as though the infant to be fonted
instead were to be interred.

And indeed the service (unexpected as had been
the birth itself) seemed haunted
if not quite as I hinted,
for firstborn so late less a boon
might prove than bane.

But despite fears he might turn stubborn
he made not the least fuss
until his face
under the water that is dipped each babe in
seemed on a sudden to burn.

For the liquid steamed and even the parson fainted
when in a warning voice
that rang inside the holy vase
Euhoe! he cried, Euhoe! as he vented
(though that may have been unintended)

over the holy man, who not at all offended
restored thus from his faint
round the slopping font
in wreath of stone and belly still more distended,
with transformed bystanders banded,

danced to an organ pipe. Meanwhile the well oiled babe
cool and counter to the hubbub
swam till my head span,
then changed the water, in the tub,
with one part mother's milk to sillabub
for all to bib.
Whereat I yielded and ladled away with my spoon.

"*I must devise*"

I must devise an image of my pain
once shape size source are known. The source is fear
(thousands of fears), the shape and size are me,
the whole not like a bespoke parasite
ubiquitously battening on me, but
I inspiring on approval through my lungs,
familiar countenanced at my own meat,
and each dictated act enlarging like
a film trailer's expressionless hyperbole
from not some goat stance in the ravined brain
but its own special correspondent fear –
which makes for confidence.
                      The country's trade
under the occupation is in pain,
which, rivalries and opposites absorbed,
now acts as their sole representative
in kindest compensation.
                         And of this fool-
proof most incorruptible monopoly
I am the trademark which I must devise.
That known it needs only to be reborn.

The Deformed Transformed

(1)

Curtains on common starling cap-a-pe
roomdark to sunstage opening, there it was.
Perpendicularity of purple
crocus within the willow ring's drop scene
of sallow tenting tied capillaries
by random bluetit ribbons blue green yellow,
or cut through laser from a chromium car –
nothing to it, nothing.
                        Lifelong awaiting
the unknown bird from branches of my dream
in three pure colours to step out into my cage –
colour apart, sole dream to stay unchanged
from bird-struck far-back set in aviaries
of fact and cards nesting in cigarettes,
pretty as eggs and Amazonian tales –
and here it is, a burnt plumpudding stare,
so tranced heraldic that it can outstare
the sending sun into a stampede skid
over these polyhedral surfaces,
spilling contiguous spectrums at each slip
bent round like lotus leaves, peacocks all eyes,
coiling rainbows into the tightest curls
a tomthumb conch can spin.
                   How could this fixed
and taper elegance invest a bird
absurd as pebble-paddling ancients, Janus-bobbing
brown paper screw blown and encroaching on
all the world's lawns; and how my dream exorcised
realised now once and for all descend
with all the deliberation of a masque
from that recessed primordial perch into
this shifty nondescript?

Snap my gold cage
on this poor daily prize, prison itself
to some built in desire the sun lets out
once a drab age in a transformation scene.

(2)

The fields themselves too little occupied
in March sunshine. Where are the sleeking herds?
Winter-byred still? The duffled flocks? Extinct
with coney and Percheron? No heat of hares
like silent jets in tight formations swerving
and re-aligned to rules subtler than *Go*?

Unseen even birds, muted or dead, the few
rookery caws posthumous yet remoter
than heaven, the headline special to which sector,
a helicopter drilling decibels
into the hill-top gravestones (Where are the silent
the swifter hares?). Hutments the only crop
aboveboard here – Have crops moved indoors too?

Yet outdoors Ram and sunlight predicate
some seasonal relentment even in
a Roman solitude, and bricked upright in
by urban hibernation, cattle rocking
incredulous through the opening gate of Spring,
into high summer memories race the senses
relieved by rolling vistas to invest
this scalped bone with al fresco dewlap tall.

Renewal of a sort, but – rebirth? No
mother's glass through iron ground these acres, no
restorations across the withheld ages
of lost and tossed ones by the mages. Only
for me recognisance of alteration
by contrast, default, polar inclination
not mine. No poignance struck from tabula rasa,
a lake of speedwell speeding up a lawn,
ramping the façade like a misfit carpet,
the pampered, ampled, only nursling there.

Yet later still sunk as the sun at heel
and all as out of mind my glance caught disengaged
on blackthorn ditchjags, doggo but undisguised,
green but with weather, black but not with rot,
passed on by spike to spike that were branch trunk and twig,
eased by oblique descent into the bottoms,
quiet little pools white with the dayround dusk,
content there childishly to loiter until snatched
up in the sky-reared sky-clear eagre of complete recall.

For this arrest of life by rooted lifeguards
criss cross in depth defence from all annoys –
sun, noise, aggressor, or chance slip – though bare
equally bare of burgeon in its narrows
as that great broad without, is stacked as high
with boyhood expectation as with thorn:
– of treasure by the depository Spring
only to be known, and me; seedlings incog; odd-
mattered or -made nests; new fins at the old work
in inchmeal soundings: – treasure anticipated
or just the pleasure itself of looking: –
these evoke quaint and ancient promises
all that the bare-boned cupboard lacked achieved –
call back to prime.   So little then is needed,
as between nude and naked, to put things right;
or seemed alas to the new made over boy.

Safe Transference

Out of encompassing windows waking
into the summer dawn from grounded sleep
eyes shiver naked on the edge of all
those aromatic spouts and ringing cascades
in dread of battery and inadequacy.

But like a world on a gold pendant hanging
crystalline rondures of the light bulb hold
safe safe the polar window nodes, the whole
exploding summer, and the humming fly
switching his orbits like a boy in the
commensurate fairground of his dreams awaking.

Arable Birds

Rooks four in Fortyacre fine and seeded
parcel as much and part of its scored as for
bird music recessions as though themselves
disced and drilled in nevertheless dominate
determine are a dimension or two
of it, of that great tilted tilth, whereas
so close so white this dove remains a mite,
the widow's maybe, nevertheless a mite.

– Each rook a neutron in its standard pack
of lebensraum throughout the universe,
being indeed that same c.c. of space
folded upon folded upon itself
till volume becomes mass just within sight
– conception, rather – of the shortest rule
creation can expect to mete or rap with.
So smallest matter is a labyrinth
or view, of space.
                For blacks, as artists know,
blacks browns can bearlike (and a speckle of white)
lick the Great Boyg itself to solid shape –
that outside inside from which colours fly
like gold leaf from a pineapple of stone
in a March wind bossing the emblemed vault
of an antique conduit anxious to relume
lapsing significance with enamel glosses.

Pike

Oh, quoth the Dragon, with a deep Sigh,
  And turn'd six times together,
Sobbing and tearing, cursing and swearing
  Out of his Throat of Leather;
Moore of Moore—Hall, O thou Rascal,
  Would I had seen thee never;
With the Thing at thy Foot, thou hast prick'd my Arse gut
  And I'm quite undone for ever.

As a boy of that name, and I as young,
gave me my death then neither sentence is
nor name impossible. Pike strike by kind,
totem tag or fish, men carry a death
like a chamois spud for luck for charm
in pockets in lockets and mine a kick
sealed between wind and water gave me all
the paralysed the necessary time
to read the policy and sigh and sign
so early on for life. Cognate or cause
of millionth or birth scream, best when young
and old enough to recognise the print
with Crusoe's terror but a reader's pleasure –
five dinted Oes of death to vindicate
decades of quickset stockades at his back
gestalt, official stamps and brands of fear
honoured in every land.
                    Latent then pike
and feet retreat. Rare sighted tin lid eyes
flat flanged impervious targets signalise
as traffic beacons do safe conduct, good
cheer pale aperitifs on silver trays,
anniversaries of the compact of the groin;
– others, revivals of the first night hit,

44

as when I must jump more than inches down
and with the comic safety of the clown
walk off belowdecks unhooked from the bridge.

Now no more tokens, manifestations,
grace granted deferments, demand reminders,
kisses of death, present themselves as for
the signatures that eke out covenants,
vicarious still validation comes: –
our first cry is (I read) for air our first
breath all for death, we fill death like balloons
with breathlessly expected shapes, our shapes;
some perverse seekers suck their death blow in:
– notional these, not rounded games way darts
from bouncing paws, but all told to endorse,
like follow up or phasing out for some
Operation Mercury in medicare,
traders in cod, police checks, odd servicings,
feckless indulgent ministry of pike.

"The Universal"
or
Popular Science

The Universal was as much the first
vacuum machine as it will be the last
will be in fact the universe at least.

By some patent device or knack, difference
that blows prestige into supremacy,
it needs nor wheels nor shaft but stops at home,
all stomach inside and all stomach out,
and all in sight or flight drops in. Mass falls
gas falls, light years and passing light pitch
into the pit and fail to reappear,
tick atom particle ray wave or charge
from this dark dock of space never to emerge.

Most of the universe, mages aver,
is in this hole or worse, of galaxies
the furthest off now lacks such size our eyes
could track it were it young we old enough,
the rest could use a hundred eyes instead
of two for instant view, our milky way
would floodlight night and day, but (mentors fear)
must render as it is ten score a year
of the best suns, our suns, to the clueless maw
of some good neighbourhood minotaur.

                                        Yet
the remainder hardware in that bankrupt sky,
though good for only twopence in the pound,
still meets foreseen demands, and mages give
answers truer than accounts, as witness, poor
Pluto at every census loses mass,
descends from God to Oberon the yob,
a moon that Neptune lost and not his peer.

and will decline by decimation, if
scales refine still, into his own avernus,
annihilated by bad sums and not
the wary wavy wars of collapsed stars
stripping the gravitation each from each
as in a pane a wasp through pointed arches
of a crane fly thigh crunches after thigh.

Mass breakage too is no more astronomical
Universal than in life's small family firm:
an annual investment in creation,
each individual daily act with means
to overpopulate the earth, a birth
at most, most often nought, for sole return,
sees crawl from that black cul de sac, for all
the thousand worlds like a wet booted ball
spuming with spunk shot in, or that one life
itself good but for nothing: null or nil.

If so small nature inconceivable
energies of unconception can accept,
the Black Death pitting the whole universe
may die itself before its stellar hosts
of swollen belly with the winds of nothing;
or the bubbles of this colic, this Nirvana,
articulated by their radiation, be
templates and temples of new masses so
mass may be nothing finding its own form
in measurements too negative for rule,
and time takes such a tumble as to serve
not even as a humble bracket curve
in the equation of negation with creation,
or the convenient lettering of a line
in the pure geometry of empty space.

But while the dear old Universal drives
the big game milling in its bag, pelt flesh
horn roar callow or hoar, svelte warded bone,
yet shakes no emptied Humpty Dumpty out
or vanished grin but (for these magic days
theories proliferate as the poem writes)

the latest cry in the last materials – bales
in a trice like an ice in the larruping
tongue of an allover Disney dog cas-
cading into a smoke of veils, so keeps
far hence still chained the Fenris Wolf, – less chance
ill chance attends the macrocosm out-
riding on honed edges ages full
of red leech cups only to be about
to be sepulchred in this droning hoover,
the microcosm's last fling and break through,
most pileate housepride that must tidy at
all costs saving its own, clean nouveau riche
sweeps all before it in the common ditch
so cocksure of its everlasting niche
earthquakes are not unwelcome now and then
provided thickest in thickest walks of men
to make new rooms or brooms; or as Keats said
"What a pity, Haydon," (exclamation-marked
with the alpha plus of genius by whom)
"What a pity there is not a human dust hole."